Essays of Night and Daylight

Undoing a Divided Nation

PJ Temple

Temple Press

Copyright © 2018 by PJ Temple

All rights reserved. No portion of this book may be reproduced in any form without permission from the publisher, except as permitted by U.S. copyright law. For permissions contact: www.pjtemple.com.

The events in the book are my memories from my perspective. Certain names have been changed to protect the identities of those involved.

Cover Photography by PJ Temple

Printed and designed by CreateSpace

ISBN 978-1-7325547-0-2 (Paperback)

www.pjtemple.com

Table of Contents

Foreword Flash 6
Introduction 8
Why I Write 9
Part 1: The Ominous They 17
Oh, Boy! 19
Oh, Like You Wear a Dot on Your Head? 26
Oh! That's Why You're so Down 29
What Are You? 34
You Speak Such Good English 37
Faces in Search of Saviors to Blame 42
Illusions of Next Time 50
Don't Kick Books 58
Girls Gone Wild: The India Footage 61
Pick One, Dang It 65
Ridiculous Lessons I Learned from my Indian Parents ... 70
Part II: To Conquer Nothing 72
The Typical Bar Scene 73
Too Dark to See 76
Be Cool 80

Thank You, Mr. Heye	87
Am I A Sociopath?	94
UIC Indian Wars	99
I Pledge Allegiance	106
What Sharing Privilege Looks Like	110
Grief of a Female Immigrant	115
Black Magic	126
Spirals	129
We Are Conquistadors!	131
Part III: Ground Me Without Stepping on My Mind	134
Being the Wrong Kind	137
The Symbiosis of Dowry	145
Grandma's Bad Ass Tattoo	150
The Chai Alchemist	155
Acknowledgements	157

Foreword Flash

You know how authors usually have someone real influential say in the foreword how legit and fabulous the author is and how important the book? I didn't do that. Instead, I'm going to tell you a story.

I was at the park jogging one spring evening as the sun was setting. Some random guy walks across the park, comes up to me and says, "Hey, do you like to write?" What kind of a question is that? Do I like to write? Picture a three-year-old pigtailed child running frantically after a paleta cart through Chicago's Little Village. For me, that's writing. That 3-year-old was also me, and I still sometimes do that.

But anyway, I slow down my jog but keep it moving and casually slide my finger over my mace, perfectly in position to spray this guy up real ugly. Yet, I was also intrigued. How in the world would he know that?

"Yeah," I yell real tough with as much bass in my voice that I could gather.

He replies, "Cool, cool. God told me to tell you that you're going to be a writer one day." I figured I better get started. I didn't need a more reputable influence.

Introduction

One of the most powerful ways we can undo injustice is by sharing our stories. I share some of my stories of culture, inequity and perceptions of American life through the lens of a woman of color.

In Part I, I focus on culture and how it impacts us, both in subtle interactions of everyday life and throughout our being, whether for good or evil. In Part II, I write about the complexities of privilege and racism. Part III highlights the mistreatment of females, and our magnificence despite it.

Something important changes as we hear each other's stories. We hear threads of similarity. We hear joy, pain, struggle and strength. We hear ourselves. Thank you for reading.

Why I Write

For a long time now, I've felt helpless about how poorly people treat each other. Like, why are so many children being shot down while playing at the park or standing in front of their homes, sometimes by civilians, other times by cops? I couldn't come up with answers on how to stop it. I felt like it was so much bigger than what one person could do.

I wished there was a tangible way I could be part of some type of solution. But what could I, someone with very little power, do? I'm a woman. I'm a minority. I'm a hanging-by-a-thread middle class American. I don't have the power or financial resources to make a tangible change.

But you know what I realized I had? God. And you know what God gave me? The desire to write. Ever since I remember being in school, I remember wanting to write obsessively. In second grade, I won a spot on the young authors winners' list, maybe because it was an interesting story, maybe because I was contending with only two other kids. I honestly don't remember. But I do remember my teacher beaming as I presented my piece to the school about a boy lost in a forest.

My parents came. They saw. They shrugged. They asked each other, "What does writing stories have to do with being a doctor?" Unwittingly, my dream was tainted. But as any desire divinely commissioned, the longing to write was relentless.

The stories resurfaced. Teachers' wide smiles kept my hopes brightly lit. I kept writing and writing. And naturally, the teenage years gave me plenty of material. *I gotta write this rap,* I'd say to myself.

My parents have me trapped.
They're wack.
I think I'm gonna crack.

I didn't say it was profound writing. I was simply throwing (up) my emotions onto paper. It was quite wretched. But I kept writing.

And oh man, did I have something for those secret boys I couldn't tell my strict parents about, the boys who broke my tender little high school heart. Oh yes, I took my revenge. With words.

Stupid boy
What a punk
You smell like funk
Anyway

Again, not my most powerful writing but it didn't matter. Justice had been served.

Whatever I was thinking had to be slammed onto paper until my mind's inkwell was dry, sometimes for relief, sometimes for sanity. And speaking of my scary little Indian parents, they were so strict and so, so… I don't know, Indian, that I didn't have room to think or breathe. So naturally, I had to start a secret journal, one that had masked sayings of how miserable it was being a teenage Indian who was born in America and living with the worst parents ever. Or how it sucked to have parents who I thought hated me.

Maturity is a great thing and it's good to learn that it could've been worse and they didn't actually hate me, but they hated that I loved American ways, and especially American boys. They were terrified of those *crazy ass Americans*. I was American.

When I met the boy I'd love forever, it was the best thing that happened. It was the worst thing that happened. My parents would never accept him or anyone I chose. They already had someone in mind. They were planning an arranged marriage for me since I was four, so what did it matter what I thought? I wasn't supposed to have my own thoughts anyway.

But every moment I was with him was every moment I knew it couldn't be. It was beautiful. It was a whirlwind. It was a hot mess. We wanted forever. It was impossibility. I could never receive my parents' blessing to commit my life to someone they didn't choose.

He wasn't an Indian, Christian, tall, fair skinned, handsome doctor from the exact region that my family originates from in India. I could never in a million years bring home an American, a black American, a black American musician. But as it turned out, after nearly two years of hiding him, I couldn't hide him anymore. Well, I could, but only for a good two more months at most, before my belly would betray me.

It was all very tiring. It was time to let go of my silly attempts to appease an unforgiving culture and finally find peace with my decisions. Before then, I deluded myself for a long time, pretended I was going to be an obedient daughter and meet my parents' many expectations. I just wasn't that conforming. I was a stubborn jerk. I had always been. And being me made the whole debacle even more difficult. And that meant I was overwhelmed. So I did what I always do when I'm sad and confused about weird life stuff. I wrote it all down.

It started as a twenty something page essay about my relationship with my secret boyfriend, Kevin, my conservative parents, and the whole hot mess of straddling multiple cultures. I wrote about how when Kevin and I first met, we had to duck and hide, sometimes literally, from view. I wrote about how Kevin thought it was all very bizarre and pointed out how I was an adult and still getting whooped for coming home late.

I wrote about a lot. And then I paused. For almost twenty whole years. And then I picked up the essay and reread it. And then I realized there was far more to write about.

What about the rights of women and the way things were in India, about choice as an Indian woman in America? What about arranged marriage, bride burning and the rape culture? What about the state of race in America and how the hell was it ever going to get better with such insidious apathy from the many people of color who felt they don't have the power needed to create change? And what does biracial even mean in our country? What have I done to my kids?

I used to laugh about the insignificance of movies. *What's the point of a bunch of stories? Some aren't even true. And who cares if they are? They're just stories.* And then I wrote one. And I read many. These stories made me realize that people's narratives have transformed lives, sometimes saved them. They can illustrate humanity in a way that creates bridges, reaching out to the corners of people's hearts. And I realized that my writing is my platform, to do something differently so that I might paint a picture of why black lives matter, why so many immigrants try to rid themselves of their accents like leprosy, or to simply make the point that no human is subhuman.

Each of us is powerful. Each of us can catapult change, each with the affinity given to us, that undeniable drive that keeps us up half the night and makes us jump out of bed dreadfully early. And that's why I write.

Part 1: The Ominous They

Tyrion, a fearless man who perpetually battles many odds, offers telling words to live by as he refers to a frightful yet elusive force – *they*.

Tyrion: "Podrick."

Podrick: "Yes, my Lord."

Tyrion: "They'll be following you now."

Podrick: "Who will?"

Tyrion: "I don't know. They, they, the ominous THEY.*"*

– Game of Thrones

Tyrion alludes to the reality that *they* are an ill-defined bunch. Yet our achievements and fears are so often driven by relentless worry about what *they* might think or say. But ultimately, outside of the people who are most precious to us, the others have little impact on our life decisions. They may have opinions but they have no real impact.

How many times have we allowed some warped image of *they* to grow into an all-powerful force in our imagination and stunt us from birthing a new idea or relationship? We ask ourselves, *What will people think?* Well, they're going to think whatever they want to think. They'll probably think a lot of things, in fact.

But the more important question is, will that change how you live? What will you do? Will you do what *they* want or what you've been dreaming of? *They*, while ominous and oppressive will continue to wallow and flail in their misery and customs. But you and I... we will move forward and be curious, creative and beautiful in spite of it.

Oh, Boy!

I had to be about four years old because when I was five, we moved someplace else. Dad and I were walking out of the apartment to pick up Mom from work. I had my pajamas on under my winter coat and a scrunched up sleepy face.

We'd drop Mom off at the department store where she worked the second shift. Then, Dad and I would come home, eat dinner, pray and go to sleep. At what felt like the middle of the night, we'd get back up and leave to pick up Mom. It was probably somewhere about 12 am, but of course, that *is* the middle of the night for a kid.

Dad told me I had to find my dumb striped scarf before we left. I was annoyed, maybe even a little disgruntled, but it made a lot of sense. Winter in Chicago at 12am is not nice. It's like pins sticking you in the face as you move through the unforgiving cold. Walking faster just turns the pins into daggers. And running makes you feel like you're standing still, encased in a frozen block of ice. The effects of winter in Chi Town are weird and cruel and have probably thrown many residents into some parallel time warp.

I looked everywhere and couldn't find the scarf. All I wanted was to get the pick-up over with so I could go back to sleep. I finally found it under my bed, which was collectively me, Mom and Dad's bed, actually. We lived in a one-bedroom apartment.

All through my childhood, Mom would remind me of how when she was little, Mom, her older brother by a year or so, and my grandma would all sleep in the same bed. She shared this with great enthusiasm, as though she were describing a remote tent camping excursion.

In fact, everything my parents talked about when discussing India was said with excitement and pride. And it was almost always compared with the

American version. It could be anything at all. Indian food was far more superb than American food. Indian clothes were well made and would last a lifetime, as though I'd want to wear the same clothes for a whole lifetime.

The people were immensely better than Americans and far more prudent. My parents would go as far as to pretend that all people of Indian origin were collectively so pious that they were completely ignorant about sex, even to the point that any American mention of it was terribly offensive. "No one talks about these things except these shameless Americans," they'd say. I mean, even the water was magnificent. It was utterly stupendous. It was clear and tasted like candy and gave you superpowers.

But see, I visited India as a young child, and if I remember correctly, the most frequently heard topic was someone always cautioning somebody else to boil the water first. "Make sure you boil the water first, okay? Make sure!" My parents never talk about that part though, the part where it's boiled almost to the point of total evaporation, probably sterilized and maybe even prayed over a couple times before being ready for consumption.

I rubbed my eyes as we finally walked out of our apartment. Although, as I sluggishly shuffled out of the door, I happened to accidentally step on my ugly scarf.

"Oh boy!" I said and began dusting it off resentfully.

Dad, who was locking the door, swung around in shock, almost stabbed himself with the key from whipping around so fast, crinkled his eyebrows and said slowly through clenched teeth and a more pronounced accent than usual, "Vhat BOY?"

"No boy, Dad. No boy," I shook my head hoping to reassure him but more importantly, to flatten his anger.

"Then, vyyyyy did you say it?"

"I don't know. Taylor says it, too."

"Who is Taylor?"

"She's my friend in school."

"Oh." He looked relieved. A girl.

It's like from the moment I was born, Dad had been terrified that one day, I'd discover what a boy was. And this was that moment.

From that day on, I acted like I was thoroughly repulsed by anything affiliated with the b word. It was also the moment I realized I needed to go underground with the truth on all things even mildly American.

Forget dating a boy or even looking at one. I wouldn't even be able to refer to someone of the male gender, along with many other restrictions, provisos and addendums along the way. And they all led to having no type of American excitement at all. I think they would've had me watch TV with my eyes closed, if there were a way.

We finally headed out of the building to pick up Mom after that near fiasco. And on the way there and back, I sat in the car quietly stomping on that ugly ass scarf with all the Chicago winter nastiness that would smear off the bottom of my boots.

Dad opened the car door to help me out. "Where is your scarf? It's wery, wery cold out here." He scanned the back seat for it. It was almost unrecognizable when he discovered it in a muddy pile on the floor. He glanced at me, working up to that look he had earlier during the "oh boy" situation. I just shrugged my shoulders and jumped out of the car.

The cold punched me, pins turning into daggers. And then there I was, running toward the apartment building yet suspended too. It didn't matter if I ran or not, I'd be trapped in that block of ice either way, for years to come. Once inside the building, I turned back and looked at him through the lobby window.

Oh boy, did he look angry.

Oh, Like You Wear a Dot on Your Head?

That's how I'm recognized by some, the kind of person that wears a dot on her head. "Oh, a Hindu?" they say excitedly. Not exactly, but they're getting closer. And more importantly, they're trying. It's a lot to explain, but I do my best.

Well, I'm Christian, see, so I'm not Hindu, which is a religion. But I do understand the most frequently spoken language in India, which is Hindi. "I know it's confusing," I validate their questions and my long-winded answer for lack of a tighter definition. I try to keep it as simple as possible, but with having to decipher between Hindu and Hindi, I do get some serious eyebrow scrunching.

I don't mind the question though, not at all. People are looking for clarification. Many times, they don't know the difference between Indian, Middle Eastern and Sri Lankan. How could they? It's not like it's super easy to tell the difference. Sometimes, I'm not exactly sure what ethnicity someone is. I've mistaken Panamanians and Mexicans for Indian. Ultimately, we can't be sure of someone's race and ethnicity. So it's best to simply ask.

What was offensive, however, was when people threw stuff at me while I was driving shortly after 911. Around the same time, I heard that an Indian man was killed because some idiot mistook him for a Middle Eastern Muslim terrorist. That could easily have been me. It could've been one of my friends or family members. How can anyone tell who a terrorist is, or isn't?

I hate hate. What are people even basing their hate on when they don't know what it is they hate? If they're ignorant enough to categorize someone by looks, they're surely too ignorant to actually know what ethnicity a person might be.

So thank you to those of you who ask about the red dot and saris and Hindus and Hindi. At the end of our conversation, even if confusing, you will walk away knowing that Hindi is a language and Hindu is a person who follows Hinduism. You will know that people can be Christian and speak Hindi. You will know that the red dot is called a bindi. I know, I know, confusing and crazy and now things are rhyming. It's okay, because it doesn't have to be easy. We're complicated creatures, but beyond Hindi and the bindi, we're human.

Now, on to the next question, why do I wear a sheet as an outfit?

Oh! That's Why You're so Down

I think people really believe it's a compliment when they say it. When they find out my husband is American, they screech with excitement, "Oh, thattttt's why!" like they've been playing a secret guessing game and I'm the trivia question.

Excuse me, but, *"That's why" what,* I want to ask. Well, lots of presumptuous things, according to some. They go on to explain freely, without my prompting.

That's why you "Talk American," or "Don't have an Indian accent," or "Have that accent," or "Dress like that," or "Aren't like *those other* Indians" or "That's why you're so down."

Or this, which happens every time my one friend introduces me to someone new: "Hey guys, this is my Indian friend, Patty. She's Indian, but she's really black. Cuz she's cool." Ouch. Cool does not equal Indian ever, apparently. I love this particular friend and I know she means no harm and most importantly, totally misses the underhanded insult. So, I quietly forgive her. Every damn time.

I forgive her also because of the dumb stereotypes portrayed in the media of the stiff, Indian doctor with no bedside manner and monotone voice. In one way or another, the Indian character has some serious personality deficit. Or there's the portrayal of the heavily accented convenience store cashier who also lacks personality and wears a name tag with some version of Abu or Apu or last name default, Shah, Patel or Ali. Customers cringe as they try to get through a simple transaction of buying cigarettes because the guy's accent is as thick as cement. Sometimes, these parodies of Indian folks are so exaggerated, that *I* can't even decipher what the character is saying.

I think when most people talk about the *cool,*

non-Indian Indian person, it's not with intent to insult. It's just that people simply don't think of Indian-American me when they look at me. They see Indian, dot wearing, blingy sheet-wrapped, molasses accented, curry smelling, personality-lacking, good at math, bobble head movements-having, Indian me. I'm none of these (well, except for the bobble head thing when extra passionate about something).

People are accustomed to making rash estimations of who a person is. We make crazy ignorant assumptions in a matter of seconds. There's a reason for this. Survival. The part of the brain called the limbic system wants to know whether someone is a threat, a friend, foe, neutral, same or different.

It's the same reason women quickly assume an unfamiliar man is a potential danger. And when the limbic system is trained by ignorance, it's the reason people clutch their purses when they see a black man walking towards them. It's the reason a person is convinced her attacker was some shade of brown. It's the reason a woman on an airplane thinks the olive skinned, curly haired *ethnic* looking man seated next to her intently solving math problems is a Middle Eastern terrorist making plans to blow something up (but really it's Guido Menzio, a well-respected Italian economist). But here's the thing. The limbic system isn't racist. A frightened society is. The limbic system isn't biased. People are.

Thus, in some folks' perspectives, I'm *down* not because I was born in Chicago and grew up among Puerto Rican, Mexican, Italian, Cuban, black, white, Indian and other ethnicities. It can't be because I have friends from many walks of life, like those who were once homeless to friends who have some really phat summer homes. It's because my husband is American. The person I married suddenly defines my entire essence. Subconsciously, of course.

It's cool though (my American husband didn't

teach me to say that, by the way). I know most people don't mean to make crass generalizations. They're curious. They're fascinated by oddities such as people who don't marry within the same race or whose brown skin doesn't match their *good* English. And then there's one of my favorites, "What's your REAL name though?"

What Are You?

"What are you?" people sometimes ask, perplexed. There even seems to be frustration because when someone's ethnicity isn't identifiable, the ability to categorize is suspended.

When people ask with malicious intent, they don't know exactly how to mistreat those of us who appear more racially ambiguous. Their slurs appear feigned as if they're practicing being insulting and hurtful. It's like I have some type of fake barrier that feels almost protective because they're so silly in their attacks. It's poetic justice, their buffoonery.

But oh man, when people know exactly how they want to direct their behavior, they're heinous and ugly. It's premeditated, exact and ironically sincere. And that's the purpose the question serves for them. What they're really asking is, *what are you, so that I can hate you with a special type of ignorance.*

The "are" is sometimes drawn out and accompanied by a sneer. It's an inability to judge. Maybe they wish they could call me the N word, or maybe confidently accuse me of being an illegal "alien," or Muslim, although, if not so ignorant, they'd know that the latter isn't even an ethnicity.

Sometimes it's blatant, most times covert. On business trips, my white colleague and I were consistently pulled out of the airport security line to be frisked and have the contents of our luggage overturned. "This only happens when I'm with you," she'd marvel, as she shook her head and laughed. The perks of hanging out with me.

Most often however, the high-pitched, "What are you?" with furrowed brows and head cocked to one side is asked by well-meaning people who are simply curious. And when I tell them, they usually respond with an, "Oh! I love Indian food!" or "Have you seen Lion?" and we dive into intriguing conversations about what we are, far beyond our race. And that's beautiful because it comes from our ability to wonder and connect.

So what am I? What are any of us? Well, we're people and being human intrinsically means we're knitted in many fascinating, complex ways based on the lives we've lived. So go ahead, I see the crease in your brows. Ask me what I am.

You Speak Such Good English

Dependent on my hairstyle, I can appear racially ambiguous - short, straight, long, curly - on a particular day I can pass as Puerto Rican, African-American, South American, biracial. I love these days because people's reactions aren't as harsh as my one-ethnicity days, so instead, I might get treated as generally shitty. It's pretty entertaining because they know they don't like me but they're not sure what type of hate to go with.

Vice versa, I am dismissed by fellow Indians and get the "Why are you associating with them?" glare if I happen to be with an American friend. So I don't mind being asked where I'm from by people who are curious, although it can sometimes get a little complicated.

"Where are you from?" asks the stranger in the bread aisle.

"I'm Indian," I say, trying not to seem surprised.

"Oh! That's a coincidence. My grandmother was Cherokee Indian. What tribe are you from?"

"Um, well, not that kind of Indian, not Native American. I'm Asian Indian."

Asian and Indian are often seen as a paradox. It's perplexing for many to find that India is on the continent of Asia.

"Asian?" they ask, somewhat indignantly, almost as though I made a grave mistake about my own ethnicity, and they can't wait to correct me. "But, uh, you don't have Asian features."

"Such as?"

"Well, obviously, like slanted eyes. And you're way darker. What are you mixed with? Are you part Chinese? Japanese?"

These are such difficult conversations sometimes. I have to remind myself that it's a chance to educate.

"India is located on the continent of Asia, therefore, I'm Indian."

"I don't get it."

"Well, you know, like dot head? Hindu? Camel jack? Sand negro? Abu from The Simpsons? Gas station attendants?"

"Oh, I know, 7-11!"

"Exactly!"

"Aziz Ansari."

"Right!" *This is kind of fun, I think* to myself.

She goes on. "I would never think of him as Asian. Huh. You know what though, now that I'm getting a better look, you actually remind me of him."

What the hell? "Sorry?"

"You actually look like you could be related."

Insult? Compliment? Not sure. He's not a bad looking guy, but he's a guy. I also don't see a resemblance, except for the signature Indian dark circles under the eyes.

"Huh. Okay, you get it now. Well, nice talking to you."

I was done.

"But wait, how come you don't have an accent AT ALL."

"Don't I?"

"No. You actually speak REALLY good English. Just like Aziz. But he's an actor so he was probably trained to talk proper English. Wow, you don't have a hint of an accent. That's awesome."

I am a lover, not a fighter, but I have my limits.

"Well, that's because Aziz and I were born in Amer--- you know, actually, never mind, um, I have to go."

- Excerpt from memoir, Where the Tiger Dwells

Faces in Search of Saviors to Blame

What does it really mean to be a good little Indian girl, to be obedient and respectful? I suppose my idea of good and the idea of hypervigilantly saving face equated to subservience. It meant danger because for me, it meant vulnerability. It was a simple equation, really. Saving face equals being obedient, equals being quiet, equals being secretive, equals being injured.

It was covert. Maybe it was because of the stories I heard or the Indian movies I saw. As a kid, even in the most current movies played by the most highly esteemed actors, there were sometimes subtle hints and often, blatant suggestions, that females weren't equal. It was implied that there was something fundamentally missing within us. We were empty shells behind those fitted blouses accentuating perky breasts and snugly wrapped saris. We were void of influence and some special quality men had that was unattainable for us. It was an absolute truth and therefore not open for contemplation.

No one explicitly said this. It wasn't something that was taught along with stranger danger, don't do drugs and other scary things. Dad surely didn't raise me like that. Mom didn't intend to. Though instead of giving me messages, she lived out what was engrained in her mind. It was the little things she said like, "Girls don't dress like that. You have to wear this jewelry. Nice girls don't say that. They don't talk back."

She talked back all the time, and she still does. She talks back to Dad, she talked back to her mother and she definitely sassed all of her brothers, even the older ones. Hell, she talks back to herself, muttering about all the things that annoy her as she goes about her day. Yet, I wasn't to talk back because that's what she was supposed to teach me. She was supposed to keep me safe.

I somehow knew that saving face, which is synonymous to compliance, had great cost. It sometimes meant there were risks that couldn't be undone and that many tragic wrongs are overlooked. The protection of children for instance, particularly a girl, is secondary to maintaining an untarnished reputation. The mental and physical health of a child is devalued and the rest of the family continues a game of charades that they're too far into to stop, as if nothing has changed.

The wounded, most of all, try to go on pretending as if nothing has changed. But inside, the body reminds her that everything is different. Her sleep is fitful. Her appetite has vanished. Her thoughts are no longer hers. They are overwritten by vile memories and terror that causes her to freeze at unsuspecting moments. She is different. And her changed self is alone. This loneliness is new. Her so-called loved ones do what they've always done, which is not a damn thing. After all, she's a girl.

Instead, they selfishly try to escape the dread by escaping her. It made her lonely. They never avoided her before or pretended they were overly busy. They never avoided her gaze when she was well, intact.

She didn't want to be left alone but then again, didn't have much to say either. Where to start? What's there to say anyway? Those around her are now negligent, even calculated in their avoidance. They didn't know what to do with her silence. Yet, all she quietly yearned for was a peaceful presence. "Just be here, in the silence with me," she wanted to plead.

Maybe sometimes they are patronizing. Most times they are vicious and accusatory. Self-blame begins to suit her better than rightly placing accountability on the vicious dog that harmed her. No one knows that through her young eyes, the world is tainted and anyone outside her door becomes a wolf, lurking and waiting to attack. The chai vendor, her teacher. Anyone can be a perpetrator now.

Girls are not revered as precious, intelligent beings but quite the contrary. They are made only to appease men. So when she sees a group of grimy, glaring guys while walking to the neighborhood store, it's no longer unusual that she might sense the trickle of warm liquid slithering down her leg. She feels vulnerable and juvenile because she is once again immobilized. After so many times of feeling further deflated by this scene, she decides leaving the house is no longer necessary.

Sometimes, the wolves lurk in her own home, or in her uncle's, dressed in sheep's clothing, touting the Bible or the Bhagavad Gita and having memorized powerful scriptures. Cowering behind robes is the revered and unquestioned, carrying his esteemed title as man of the cloth. The dissonance confuses her.

No more parties. She doesn't want parties. *What kid doesn't want parties*, her family wonders. The anticipation makes her palms sweat and her pupils dilate into large saucers as the sudden drought in her throat chokes and abandons her. The dreaded secret glances at her and he's void of remorse, but rather looks on with unspoken and paralyzing threat.

It makes her question God. Is He real? If so, why has this happened to me? No one is willing to explain this heavy contradiction. No one is willing to set things right. No one has forbidden the wolf from trespassing her with his presence. No one cares to let her know God is righteous and is hurting because of the wrong done to His precious child, that free will can be beautiful, but conversely, can extinguish the soul faster than it can recover. Instead, she turns on God, blames Him for her perplexing torment. And, as she was taught that her body is the temple of God, it is most appropriate that naturally, it is she and God who are at fault. Someone must be blamed.

Concealment is the family's only viable option, and a necessary measure. Otherwise, it will diminish the possibility that the girl will be an appropriate candidate for marriage because she is now "ruined." Even if family is not the one shaming her for provoking a man to become aroused, society may in turn blame the family.

The twists and convoluted turns of society's blame. "Maybe God is punishing them because they did something they weren't supposed to, some secret thing we don't know about. Surely, someone in this family has done something very, very bad. This is God's wrath and revenge!" This leaves the perpetrator to make a clean escape through the many passageways allowed to him.

Saving face equals being obedient, equals being quiet, equals being secretive, equals being injured.

Illusions of Next Time

"Dad, I think it's a good time for me to start looking for an apartment. I'm almost twenty. I need to be more independent."

"Oh no. Vy move? You vill stay here until you get married. We don't believe in moving, boving."

He's over-rhyming. The topic must've struck a chord for him. He might as well have said moving out is hocus pocus, a mythical idea reserved for spooky nights around campfires. He made the idea sound outlandish and revolutionary. I suppose it was, in his mind. Girls don't leave home and live alone somewhere away from family. For what? It's not sensible. That's how Dad sees it. I get that.

But he doesn't get how I feel. He thinks it's just fine that a twenty-year-old be treated like a ten-year-old, that my parents tell me exactly who to marry and what career to choose. I must study medicine. It's the best field. No one gets into the field of psychology. Surely it will lead to poverty and eternal angst. What is psychology anyway? And writing, it's just a frivolous waste of time for those political types. My parents even made specific suggestions about which friends I should spend time with.

And none of this was a problem for them. They believed it was what they were supposed to do. After all, they didn't have the luxury of casually choosing the careers of their hearts' desire. They came to America, worked hard and made money to provide us with opportunities, to ensure their work wouldn't go uncultivated. Maybe a different angle would work.

"You know things have been hard. Me, you and Mom are having a hard time getting along these days. Moving out can change that."

"No, no, no!" he insisted.

That means no more discussion. It's final. And this is exactly why I had to be even more persistent.

"But Dad, I'm gonna move out eventually. And you guys didn't let me move out for college, not even to live in a dorm fifteen minutes away. How long do you think I'm supposed to stay here?"

"Vokay, vokay, I vill help you look for an apartment, vokay? Ve vill look for apartments and find out the cost and I vill help pay your rent."

Wow, better than I expected. He might've figured it was a wiser trade off than moving even further. But it was too good to be true. The day never came. We never discussed moving out again. The few times I asked about it, he responded with his often-heard response, "Next time," which really meant, "Never gonna happen," but he didn't have the emotional energy to say what he really meant.

And what did he really want to say? That tradition doesn't allow for my request, at least not in this family? That if I went off to live on my own, I would become even more Americanized than I was and make a complete mess of my already disoriented life? That I might run off and become a heathen who abandons the love and protection of God and morals, and all the righteous ways of good Indian culture?

He'd have an endless list of criticisms, I'm sure. Was he being controlling, unreasonable, and maybe even emotionally stunting my young adult growth? Most definitely. Would he be willing to face these facts and talk them through with me? Absolutely not. Talking is frivolous and accomplishes nothing. Processing emotions is a waste of time. Expressing yourself is for Westerners.

Instead, his way was to quietly pretend nothing difficult was happening and hope that if he ignored the problem, it would disappear. So it was often that the elephant just hung out in the room while we skirted around it. He once told me that in Indian culture, many things are unspoken and rather assumed. I get that. At times, we're an outwardly verbose, emotionally quiet culture. Yet, pretending only works for so long. Dad's ability to walk away silently was deteriorating, and would inevitably reveal long concealed rage.

But for now, he simply went to his fall back, "Next time." It was frustrating to know that "next time" was not only his default stance for all undesirable, flighty suggestions, but that next time wouldn't come. There wouldn't actually be any true consideration or mention of the idea again. "Next time," was the classier and more evasive version of, "Shut up talking about it or I'll kick your ass."

It's hard to say why my dad has usually been so superficial in our discussions. But then again, I think about how he worked so hard to maintain a decent life here and the sense of isolation he must've felt because his family was still in India.

It seemed he became accustomed to deferring his feelings, deferring his thoughts, deferring conversation or just about anything he possibly could so that he didn't have to face them. "What's talking going to do?" he said a million times. Who has time to face whiny adult children when all you know is to push forward so you can stay above water? Instead, he jokes. He jokes a lot, about small things, about big things. He jokes. He laughs. He appears happy and jolly and carefree.

For him, humor is like a whip he uses to perpetually brandish away the bad feelings, keep away the confusion of why he works so hard for an ungrateful family who has no idea how little he had in India. He used it to keep away the disappointment of what the Promised Land really had waiting for him. Where was the milk and honey?

With his whip he thrashed at the paradox that was The Land, and how rather than fulfilling its promise, it took from him, demanding he offer a sacrifice of his three children if he wanted to continue to remain in it. So, he wears his jester's mask and wields his weapon for the next time he must ward off the many disappointments that plague him.

But his deferral of all things even mildly stressful had birthed a large, looming monster that was nurtured by long-suffering, and grew strong on milk and honey. This monster, it was well cared-for, and its power could be seen only in those magnificently scary moments when he felt he couldn't endure much more. It came out baring teeth, screaming for some consolation to the madness he had endured since coming to this cold country. Coming here changed everything.

Why wouldn't he want to snugly place a facade over his tired eyes, his hoarse voice, his defeated will, and return to the protection of his shield and weapon? Once us kids grew up and moved away, what did he really have? He came here only to lose the family he so carefully created.

Don't Kick Books

One evening, maybe in the fall, because I remember a chill coming through our apartment windows, Mom was in an especially energetic mood. She tucked the long part of her sari in the waistband of her slip, and pushed her hair behind her ears. She said we'd learn a song and then maybe, if we got it down, we'd learn a couple of Indian dances, too.

"Which song, Mom?" I asked.

"Sally Had a Rat," she said, with excitement.

She was almost smiling. I didn't know that song, but I didn't care. We were going to learn a song together.

It was spontaneous. It wasn't her at all. But I liked it. First thing we did was make room. I was working on some stupid fifth grade math homework when she made the thrilling suggestion, so I pretended I was all done. We put stuff away to clear space on our plush, baby blue carpeted floor. The walls were painted blue too, very closely matching the hue of the carpeting. There was no contrast at all. Everything was the same. Everything was blue.

There wasn't much to clean up. Mom was too neurotic to leave things just sitting around. Since I was already on the floor, I just tucked things behind other things, like the sofa or under the table, just past where the tablecloth drapes down. Weirdly, she didn't even seem to notice. She always noticed. She always had rules. But for now, she was busy cueing up the song we'd learn. The cassette tape read, Solid as a Rock by Ashford and Simpson. *Sally Had a Rat,* I thought, suppressing giggles. I continued to straighten up through muffled laughter.

My books were near my feet. I extended my right leg forward and shoved the books with my foot as far as they'd go under the sofa.

"Hey! You don't do that!" she snapped. For a

moment, she was her stern self again. Instinctively, I ducked. To my surprise, she continued on. "Books are what will save you one day in this crazy, prejudice country. You never place your feet on your books. They're like the Bible."

"Sorry Mom, I didn't know," I responded weakly, my throat now dry. Yet, even as I was saying it, I had no idea what she was talking about. *They're just books*, I thought. And I went on preparing to learn Sally Had a Rat, our first song together.

Girls Gone Wild: The India Footage

Having a baby out of wedlock is bad. I'm guessing having a child before marriage is surely not celebrated in many places, but India may be one of the worst. First of all, it isn't even acceptable to allow yourself to think about someone of the opposite gender, so dating is out of the question. Despite this, I would think that many people end up doing that thing called *falling in love*. If Indian parents come to know of it, and both sets of families are agreeable to allowing the two lovebirds to marry, the outcome is usually favorable, although exceptionally rare in some parts.

It's quite the aspirational goal to meet parents' specific requirements of similar caste, status and aesthetics. "He must be smart. Smart and very handsome. He must be handsome and tall. He must surely be fair. Fair skinned, tall, handsome and smart. A doctor."

Aspirational, and maybe sometimes even impossible. "He must also be Christian. He must be a Methodist Christian from our same city in India. He must be Methodist, Christian, smart, handsome, tall, very tall, fair, so so fair, and a doctor. And he must speak Telugu. We will pray for a husband only like this for you. God will bring him."

In most cases, since dating is unthinkable, lovers have to live in shrouds of secrecy. There's the danger yet thrill of the hiding. There's the secret meetings, the customized secret code you speak when other people are around. And the reality is that most secret places and things include lots of heavy, secret sex. The next natural reality is that frequent, heavy and secret sex often leads to lots of firing off of really headstrong, fiery sperm.

This, then, halts all the excitement and raging emotions, and instead leads to the age-old dilemma of what the hell to do next. Two people who are deeply and horribly in love may quickly unravel and break apart like old, brittle bones when surrounded by the shame they must inevitably face. Only then is the fragility truly revealed. In fact, in many cases, the oh-so-in-love guy disappears without a trace. That leaves an often young, very scared woman to decide what's best.

In many parts of India, there is no such thing as an unwed mother. That's not a concept people are willing to grasp. There are no unwed mothers, liars or criminals in India according to some, um, reliable sources. It simply doesn't happen because India is just *that* perfect. It's almost heaven, well except for its poverty, lack of fair and effective government, and general chaos in marginalized areas.

So if unwed mothers did somehow exist in this perfect world, they'd be treated like ghosts, as non-existent, especially by their families and friends. In their parents' eyes, they would no longer have a daughter. The haunting fear of the future would be carried by the girl alone. In fact, if she isn't banished from her home, she and her baby may be killed for committing this heinous crime because it would bring irreparable shame to the family name. This leaves her with no alternative. Sometimes, Mama and Baby can only find safety and solace in the depths of a river, quietly sinking away as their shame is dissolved by the cleansing waters. But alas, the family name is spared as their daughter's death is vaguely explained away as a tragic accident.

Pick One, Dang It

People don't like ambiguity. It's like they're itching to yell, "Pick one already. You're confusing me." They're rarely satisfied when I explain that I'm Indian but born in America.

"So which one are you?"

"Both."

"Yeah, but which one are you MORE?"

I've turned over questions like this in my mind growing up, but more so subconsciously. It was jarring to hear it out loud. It was like even my subconscious was knocking at the door demanding some kind of resolution.

As I got older, I began to feel more balanced about the meaning and perceptions of culture. However, it was more of a feeling, not something I could easily explain. Like so many of my emotions and life circumstances, it hovered right above my subconscious. If I were to face it all head-on, I suppose my mind would be a mangled mess.

Being American is amazing. Kids are encouraged to explore their needs at a rather early age. At age nine or ten, the American child is learning about identity and autonomy, exploring what she wants in life as an individual. American parents often nurture these interests. Discussions are not about what a child must do but rather what she is interested in doing. "Honey, would you rather play volleyball or tennis?" It's not uncommon to hear American children talk about rights and deserving respect.

Despite embracing the individualistic culture of America, I've also grown to appreciate that living in a collectivistic society has its benefits, even if that means my parents disagreed about how many rights I actually had. In Indian culture, everyone is family. That includes far removed aunts, uncles, neighbors from The Old World and their neighbors' neighbors'

neighbors. Extended family is pretty synonymous to nuclear family. If you need something, you have a hundred different people you can call.

Minor down side: if you're a teenager whose parents don't approve of the reckless things you're doing, expect droves of family members to visit with advice and embarrassing threats, like, "If you're doing the drugs, I will call the police. If you're talking to a boy, I will beat you and then I will call the police." The only up side to this down side is that whenever two or three or fifty gather, there's always food, even in times of crisis. Especially in times of crisis. We're a culture of emotional eaters.

There are other good things too, like portability of family support. If there are sub-clans of family in Kansas who you may know of but haven't actually met, there's still a good chance they will welcome you into their home.

If someone becomes a widower and is left with children to raise, the arranged marriage track is very beneficial. Just pick up the phone and put a smoke signal out to the matchmakers, and a mission commences for a suitor who isn't opposed to a lovely woman who comes with a couple of toddlers. In more traditional times, that widow may not remarry, but in more practical times, it's arranged marriage's finest hour.

The idea of having a village with you feels reassuring. We take up a lot of space and we have an unintentionally loud and imposing presence, laughing heartily with high-pitched tones and talking busily in an Indian dialect sprinkled with English. We speak Telugu, so Dad calls it Tinglish. It's one of his worst Dad jokes (and shouldn't be counted as a joke at all), but also kind of cute. Even though all of this is going on, we're often oblivious of our caravan's obnoxious banter.

That's just how our village operates. It's like there's a permanent safety net that will never fray or break, that is, if you're fortunate to have a family who is forgiving. Despite the horrible words my parents hurled at me over the years, and aside from their retaliation as they felt the pain of my cultural betrayals, the safety net refused to break. It may have swung violently for a while, and it may have felt like it was going to give, but in the end, it was still there. Why would I want to relinquish the unconditional protection of my family? Who says I have to pick?

Ridiculous Lessons I Learned from my Indian Parents

- Mad respect to chai. Learn to make it and everything else in life falls into place.
- Spankings are bonding time.
- They're not actually mad when they yell. That's just how they talk.
- You're not Indian, you're American, that's until you want to do American things like hang out with friends til 1am. Then they're like, "Indians don't go outside after 9pm." Hmmm. I didn't know there was a special Indian curfew.
- It's not *turn off the light*, it's *off the light*. It's not *turn off the TV*, it's *close the TV*. Keep up.
- Grades define who you are, but don't worry, that's only until you're an adult. And then it's

your career. By the way, sports and art are dumb.
- Always wear super shiny clothes no matter where you're going.
- When you're walking around the grocery store with your really shiny Indian clothes and people stare, you're supposed to yell, "Hey! Vat the hell are you looking at?!"
- Stare back at people really hard whenever the opportunity arises because all Indians have this amazing genetic affinity for it. And don't worry, you're guaranteed to win a dirty look stare down contest any day. Boom.
- Don't make fun of your parents' accents for more than 2 minutes straight because even though they laugh along for a while, they'll eventually get super offended: "Vy are you making the fun? Ve talk beautiful English."

Part II: To Conquer Nothing

The irony of racism is that it is the exact opposite of what we need in order to conquer. Not divide and conquer. Conquer. Together and conquer. Separately, we fall. Separately, we fail.

The Typical Bar Scene

I met a few friends at a bar for a birthday thing. I hung out for a little bit. It was a nice time, but I had to go to another event. So after about an hour, I said my goodbyes and made my way to the exit. As I was leaving, the bouncer asked if I was coming back in, probably so that I could get a stamp to reenter. Close by, there was a line forming with another guy checking IDs. I told the bouncer no, I wouldn't be coming back in. And to this, a woman waiting to show her ID yelled, "Yeah, you better not be coming back in," and repeated this a couple of times, progressively getting louder and more emphatic, making sure I was able to hear. Her friends began to laugh and started yelling out something too, but because I was walking away, I couldn't make out what they were saying. And I was glad.

Here are the facts: I was at a bar on the north side of Chicago. Every single person in the bar was white except for me and a slightly ambiguous looking biracial guy with dreamy Jesse Williams' type eyes who could pass as white. I knew him, which is the only reason I knew he was biracial.

Every person standing in line to get into the bar was white. Bartenders, white. Everyone on the street outside of the bar, walking, jogging, biking, driving, whatever, you guessed it. White. Not shocking. Chicago is known for its distinct color lines, literally divided by streets.

The next time I saw my friends who were at the bar that night, including Jesse, I told them what happened. Their reaction: No! That couldn't have happened. They weren't talking to you. They meant something else by it, you know cuz the bar was getting full. They were probably drunk. Maybe they were kidding. What? Now, why couldn't they simply have said that it just never should have happened?

Too Dark to See

He was the uncle who gave me toys I actually wanted, like my first set of Mattel cars at five-years-old. I slid the perfectly molded white plastic sheet out of the box that encased a colorful selection of cars. The cars were different makes and models, and they were all mine. He knew me so well. He wasn't a blood relative but he hung out with my parents so much that he had entered the annals of honorary uncles.

He was also my most *favorite* uncle because of his thoughtful gift giving skills. Just like a kid, superficial. But was it? Everyone else assumed I wanted baby dolls, nail polish and most annoying of all, Barbies, with their anatomically incorrect body types. I once heard that if a woman were actually built like a Barbie – all breasts, no booty – the poor thing would capsize face first.

Uncle was a cool dude. He wore bell-bottoms like my parents, mainly brown or orange ones. He was in America studying to become a pastor. He often talked about his wife and kids back home longingly, and how he'd go back to India one day. He once told me I reminded him of his daughters.

Eventually, Uncle did return to India. He became a preacher there and had a fulfilling ministry. He'd call sometimes, always asking about me, his surrogate daughter. He also began to visit Chicago every few years and would camp out at my parents' house for a few days during his trips.

One day, when I was about sixteen years old, I walked in after school and there he was, a bright eyed, coffee skinned man who had become plump over the years. He lit up when I walked in. But then, without warning, his face lost its softness. He drew in a breath as his eyes squinted quizzically and he gasped, "Oh, what happened to your color?"

I laughed, taken by surprise that this would be the first thing he'd say after all this time. I felt embarrassed too, without knowing why. I was never ashamed of my skin color, even when Mom pointed out throughout the years, "You're getting so dark," dragging out the word dark every time, as though in amazement.

Apparently, I no longer met Uncle's expectations of the person he knew, the fair, sweet, good child. How devastated he seemed, as though I sinned in a way that couldn't be absolved. Growing up, he'd tell me he bragged about me often to everyone in India, about how fair I was. As a kid, I guess I only heard the first part.

Again, he marveled, shaking his head and asking, "What happened?" as though he were trying to piece together the events leading up to a terrible car wreck. I was now a mystery, maybe sinister, an untrustworthy girl. I was now an anomaly, all because I was the wrong color. Color. Darkness. Bad.

Be Cool

My 4-year-old daughter once said to someone, "I don't want to have to tell you to shut up." I know. It's terribly disrespectful. And she was at an age where it could no longer come off as cute or funny. I was ashamed. Had I somehow taught her to disregard her elders?

But I knew it wasn't that. I always taught her to be kind and spare others' feelings when able, especially her elders. I mean, I took it to an extreme, too. If an old lady came up to me and punched me in the face and smacked me with her big ole' purse for no reason, I'd start to talk smack, like, "Hey, what did you do that for, you—" and then realize what I was doing, feel dumb, apologize profusely for being rude and awkwardly run away.

But the person my daughter was speaking to was a testy somebody who often had nothing but hurtful things to say. This woman was crass, insensitive and bewilderingly narcissistic. Rather than call my daughter rude, I'd like to think of her as intuitive in this instance. Yes, she was reprimanded for being disrespectful, but I was also secretly proud that she was learning how to see truth from bullshit. And the only way I could fairly navigate this was to remind her to be cool. Over time, she understood what this cue meant. But me, I'm having a bit of a hard time with taking my own advice right now.

When Trump was first elected, I figured, hmm, maybe somehow, some way I can remain respectful. I deluded myself, thinking that there was a needle's eye of a chance that he'd do a good job. I hoped his campaigning was as gimmicky and crass as it was going to get. He would act presidential soon. He'd have to. So I prayed and I hoped that God would change Trump so drastically that the transformation itself would be proof of the existence of a higher power. But then, very fast and furiously, things got real. Real ugly.

I continued to pray, of course, probably more regularly than I had in a while. But I also struggled with how fundamentally opposed I was to the political shifts taking place with the new presidency. It was time to take action. However, I kept reminding myself that this presidency is something God allowed, for whatever reason, so I wanted to go about advocating in a respectful way. I wanted to resist, but peacefully.

But the more I tried to be respectful, the more ridiculous Mr. Trump was getting. And in result, the more I wanted to say, "Don't make me have to tell you to shut up." I'm really struggling with maintaining respect and avoiding calling him a funny-wigged, odd-face-making such and such. I really don't want to believe he can be as narcissistic and obtuse as he portrays himself to be.

But after it's all said and done, and he has already said and done plenty of goofy things, I have to be realistic. Because if I don't, I won't be advocating objectively for the rights of the many people he is isolating. Now, that doesn't mean I have to call him out on his weird, fragmented, nonsensical manner of speaking or be disrespectful in any other number of ways, but I do have to acknowledge the blatant harm he is causing to many people.

I'm a Jesus loving democrat who believes that God made some folks who are intersex or might genetically be boys but look like girls on the outside. I'm a democrat who's somewhat conservative, because none of it is that easy or that black and white. How do you try to lock down someone's perspectives and beliefs into rigid categories? It's something short of impossible. And division conquers nothing.

The essence of America is in fact that we are very difficult to categorize. Which is why the hypervigilant focus on separation is asinine. It's at such an extreme that due to the current president's biased views, even resisters are attempting to categorize. Ironically, resisters are fighting division with more division.

I am a resister. I will likely resist most of what is offered in this joke of a presidency. However, I also sometimes need to redirect the anger boiling up inside of me. I must be careful with what I do with my anger.

Is it necessary to call names, to hate the ones that hate us? That's not very Jesus-like. It's gang mentality-like. Are we going to retaliate every chance we get until unending conflict takes lives along the way, of death of body and spirit?

What are we even doing right now? It seems we're sometimes fighting fair and sometimes just fighting. Sometimes, we're attempting to repel hate with hate, which never works. Most resisters probably don't even believe in starting wars. Yet here we are fighting ideology but left with no productive communication.

Be cool, friends. Let's try to stay respectful and dignified, even if others aren't. Even if others are resentful, ignorant or just plain old bitter that we've had an eloquent, intelligent 44th president for eight years, and even when some are emboldened by a pitiful 45th presidency, resist the temptation to fight back with rage.

I'll be honest. It's hard not to stoop down to the level of a 4-year-old right now, albeit an intuitive one. It's very difficult for me not to talk about Mr. Trump's entitled ass and sometimes, I lose it and I do say some less than tasteful things. But for voices of reason to be heard, we have to remain sane. We can't move over to the other side. And I don't mean the Republican side. It's much bigger than that. I mean the rage-fueled, hateful dark side. So, I keep asking myself, *What would Jesus do?* And then I whisper, be cool, Patty, be cool.

Thank You, Mr. Heye

Traveling while brown can be adventurous and complex. And treacherous. And deadly. Traveling out of the country can have its own challenges because there's the absence of that false sense of familiarity. Yet even traveling through the United States can be perplexing. It's like being QBert, the video game character who would hop onto cubes yelling out nondescript curse words when he ran into some malevolent force. Where to safely hop next? How to navigate without stepping on the wrong cube and facing total annihilation? Makes you want to swear.

Going to the South is surely questionable and makes me think twice about how desperately I really want to travel. Where exactly can I go? Is it worth the risk? What are safe communities for brown people and how am I to be sure?

Despite my reservations, stately mountains and

the serenity of the dark woods illuminated only by the moon lured me south. Yet, as is usually true, the people of a place can be equally intriguing, sometimes perplexing.

"Confederate flags in souvenir shops? Just out there, waving around like they're not a slap in the face?" I said, voice cracking.

"Welcome to the South, baby!" my husband announced with pizazz and sarcasm, like a TV show host introducing his big winners.

"Yeah, but how are they selling them in souvenir shops? And shops owned by Indian people? Do they even know what it stands for?"

He dropped the sarcasm. "Honey, they're trying to make money for their families like everybody else. They don't have much choice but to sell this shit. THEY know they're in the South."

"That's shameless and weirdly ironic. I'm not shopping here."

We walked out, my husband appearing regretful for my gullibility, me with eyes welling up. We decided to try another shop.

"What! Again? And they have more shit with the flag on it than the other store."

"Every store we go to is going to be the same thing. We're not in Chicago anymore, Patty."

He seemed sympathetic to my ignorance, but I still felt indignant. "I knew it was going to be different, but this?"

I've had plenty of insults thrown at me, quite directly and without hesitation. Being hated wasn't a new thing. Society's collective acceptance of a visual representation was. It meant that there weren't enough people caring to say that this was an embarrassing way to represent their state. No one said, "Let's do away with it." Not enough people cared to say that. Not enough people cared to do anything. Enough people embraced the flag that it continues to be openly glorified. I realize that some still believe slavery is the best thing that's ever happened to this country. But to be allowed to profit off of this belief is sick. And then there are people who denounce oppression but try to hold onto the "good" symbolism of Southern pride. There's no good.

Even in Chicago, with its clearly demarcated lines, we can end up on the wrong side of town. Not the wrong side of town that's shown in the movies, with gangs and crime and bonfires in tin cans with scruffy men wearing layers upon layers of clothes huddling around a garbage can of flames.

Wrong side for us. Communities with tall, foreboding invisible barricades. "Don't go into that neighborhood. We're not allowed there," you hear parents of color warn. Sounds like the 1920's.

In March of 1997, thirteen-year-old Lenard Clark was beaten by three white teenage boys in the racially divided and mob-infested Chicago community of Bridgeport. In Chicago, in 1997. As some people who live in the vicinity of a tragic occurrence often say, "I didn't think it could happen in *my* neighborhood." Our invincible human delusions, so intensely in search of safety and predictability override sensibility all too often.

Then there's me. I'm one of the "It can happen anywhere," type of folks. The more cautious, paranoid type. Thanks, Mom. If it happened in Chicago, it can happen anywhere. It can happen on the other, "good" side beyond the dividing line of the infamous 8 Mile in Detroit. It can happen in Athens, Greece, which holds Parthenon, the home of Athena, goddess of wisdom. Yet, division and ignorance prevail.

Not shockingly, it can also happen in Brandenburg, Germany, where the former government spokesman, Uwe-Karsten Heye, once warned that those of a different skin color, "may not make it out alive." Quite ominous. Not very politically correct to say. Not coated, dipped and swirled with fancy words that may hint at an alarmingly high rate of racially motivated attacks sweetly masked in gooey lies.

Mr. Heye must be a logical, sensible man. Yet, there was strong opposition to his honesty and protection of us different-skinned people. They told him he couldn't say that any particular region of a country is a "no-go." The hell he can't. I very much appreciate Mr. Heye for the warning.

Even if he said, "Hey, people of different skin color, Brandenburg may be somewhat risky for you to visit," I might still stay away. Why? Because I value my life and gravitation toward realism. And if I decide to go despite the warning, I know I'm well prepared for the threats that might come my way.

The people who were opposed to Mr. Heye's

caution probably don't have to worry about crossing a line that may cause harm, or at the least, undue ridicule and shame. I want my information raw. Please hold the sugar. I can't afford it. Thank you, Mr. Heye.

Am I A Sociopath?

I was listening to a podcast on National Public Radio the other day while driving from Chicago to Missouri. It's a nice, tedious six-hour trip with winding one-lane roads and big trucks coming at you from the other side of the street, only a few inches from sure death. I needed something to keep me alert, especially as the sun was disappearing.

The segment was part of a series called Serial, in which a reporter investigated the possibly wrongful conviction of a young Pakistani man, Adnan Syed, who was sentenced to prison for murdering his high school ex-girlfriend, Hae Min Lee.

She was Korean, so they shared some cultural similarities, being of Asian culture. They must've easily related with each other's frustrations of their parents' stern and authoritarian style of parenting. Neither Adnan or Hae Min's parents were lenient regarding dating. In fact, Adnan's parents were adamant that Adnan should not date a girl outside of his culture, which meant she had to be of the same race, ethnicity and Muslim religion.

Adnan was caught in the endlessly complex, ever-revolving door of being the first generation American. That meant he had to live according to the customs of Pakistani life but covertly maintain an American lifestyle, because naturally, he was thoroughly both. This also meant he had to put on somewhat of a facade while in each of these worlds. Just like me.

In the Pakistani realm, he was described as a kind, giving, respectful young man who closely followed Muslim principles. This included no dating and, of course, it was understood, no ancillary activities that are assumed to come with it. Then there was the side of him that his family and mosque members didn't know about. He was that popular, charismatic, attractive guy in high school who didn't have any problem getting what he wanted from girls. And then, of course there was his beloved girlfriend, of whom his parents did not approve of once they found out.

According to the podcast, although there is no actual evidence that Adnan killed his girlfriend, he was convicted for murder and remained in prison without substantial evidence. Isn't it odd? The only point that prosecutors hung on, and which led to his conviction was the fact that he was able to live a culturally double seesaw of a life between home and school.

Prosecutors painted the guy to be a complete sociopath who had the capability of killing a young woman because he was attempting to navigate two cultures that were both very much a part of who he is. And maybe, just maybe, his conviction might have had a little something to do with the fact that he was

Muslim. I'm sure in some jurors' subconscious or very conscious minds, Adnan so conveniently and snugly fit into that big, bad Muslim terrorist stereotype. The jury even deferred prosecuting a black man, one of Adnan's friends, who reportedly had quite the shady account of what happened the day of the murder. So here we have the Muslim sociopath who was proven beyond the shadow of a doubt to have killed his ex-girlfriend.

Except that most teenagers in the world behave somewhat respectably in front of parents and then turn around and behave like they lost their silly minds as soon as they're in the presence of their friends. To add another perplexing layer, almost every immigrant child can probably attest to the reality that, like Adnan, they too, have lived this crazed double life. If not for our masquerade of duality, we'd be traumatized oddities who would never fit into the world. We wouldn't be accepted in

America because we'd be too something – too geeky, too ethnic, too eccentric. Nor could we return to the motherland and expect a warm welcome from our relatives, who would write us off as rebellious, spoiled Americans who turned our backs on our roots.

So when I heard that Adnan was actually convicted of murder for having to walk this fine balance of acculturation, it frightened me that I too, among millions of others, could be sloppily and preemptively assessed as a raging sociopath.

UIC Indian Wars

The story of Adnan Syed made me think a lot about my undergrad days, and the complex ways immigrants straddle cultures.

I was attending the University of Illinois at Chicago. There were a lot of Indians at my school. Like, a lot. It's the cheapest state school, so it makes sense. Yes, a stereotype. Yes, sometimes true.

"Kev, I'm thinking about joining an Indian club at UIC," I announced to my boyfriend.

"That would be cool. Have you looked into it?"

"Yeah. There are just so many options though. I don't know which to choose."

There was Asian Indian Club, which was the general one. Then there was the South-Asian Indian Club. I could do that one, too. There was the Muslim Club. It didn't specify Indian, but they didn't have people of other races in it, so it was kind of implied. Then there was the Hindu Club. There weren't too many non-Indian Hindu folks out there, so that's exclusively Indian, too, for the moment. I probably couldn't contribute much to the Muslim and Hindu clubs, but I'd learn more about their religion and culture. That would be cool. But then again, they might not want *me* there. Curiously, there's no Indian Christian Club. I would consider joining that one.

I just don't know which one of the clubs I'd fit into best. Maybe the more general one. But then again, I might even stick out in one of those. Sometimes, I get this creepy feeling like other Indians think I'm not Indian enough. And on top of it, I'm not dating an Indian man. And on top of that, I'm dating. And I have a lot to say about arranged marriage, stuff they probably wouldn't like too much either.

"Some of them look at me weird," I told Kev.

"Reealllly? And why would they do that?" He probably thinks I'm being paranoid. I can just tell by his stupid elongated "reealllly."

"I don't know. It's complicated. I see them meeting in the lounge for their clubs sometimes or hanging in the game room, and everyone's huddled around in these weird little clusters of sameness. And they all glare at my cousin and me. Okay, not all of them but some. Well, really, it's just this one group. They think they're some type of tough gang."

"Why would they be staring at you guys?"

"Well, we think it's because we're not 'Fresh Off the Boat,' or FOBs like them. So they hate us."

He seemed a little more interested now. "Wait, so they hate you because you were born here? That's stupid."

"Okay, maybe I'm exaggerating on the hate part, but I feel like they strongly dislike us because we're different."

He laughed. "Because you're different? You're all Indian."

"I know! See, it's complicated."

My cousin and I had tried being nice. We smiled. We said hi. They'd just glare. And there was this one burly, hairy guy who was just the worst. I could feel him smack us with his looks and whisper terrible things about us to his posse from the corner of his mouth, as they mean mugged us, too.

I could guess what they were saying. I just knew our angry FOB friends were talking about how we were wearing make-up and sleeveless shirts, or how our pants are too tight. They were bothered by the absence of head coverings or long Christiany church skirts or some other suffocating custom, reserved just for women. I knew one thing that was definitely going through their heads though. They were thinking, "Those girls think they're *so*

Americanized." We're not Americanized. We're American.

I realize I have a wild imagination and can become a tad bit paranoid at times. After all, I have robustly paranoid immigrant parents. But one day, my vividly imagined suspicions were finally justified when my cousin and I asked a couple of friends over to meet us in the school's game room for a round of pool.

As he was lining up the cue stick, one of my friends happened to get a glimpse of Bearded Beast and his posse, who were actively glaring at us. "What's with those guys? Do you know them? They're just standing there staring."

I was relieved. "Thank you! We thought it might just be us, but you guys see it too. They just hate us, that's all. Especially that one," I said and tilted my chin their way. "That's Big Bearded Beast."

I glanced at Beast as a show of stare-off retaliation. "I think he's the ringleader."

"Well, they make it so obvious, like they want you to know," my friend laughed.

"That's what we were saying!"

If only there were a club for American-born Christian South-Indians from Chicago. Now, they might just get me.

Ick, but wait. Was I morphing into my parents? What was this weird longing for sameness? Or was I simply grabbing for a chance at belonging. Maybe leaving the familiar is far harder than I gave my parents credit for. Makes me realize I've never been challenged to forsake the familiar in the way they have.

And that's when I had a revelation. I just wasn't the club type. So instead, I took up a tennis class where nobody cared what type of Indian I was or even what race. They just wanted to know whether I could return a ball. I finally felt like I belonged.

I Pledge Allegiance

It was my first time working in a rural town. I was thoroughly a city girl and wasn't accustomed to cornfields being my only option for a view. But there I was, learning that a slower pace isn't always a bad thing. The sounds of birds and wind rustling were different in the stillness and filled me with a kind of serenity the city couldn't offer.

Yet, on my drives to work I often marveled at just how desolate this little town was. It was like stepping back into history. Streets were often quiet, with just a few older model rusted out cars puttering down the road from time to time. You'd have to drive miles to find a restaurant, some of which were named something like Kathy's Kozy Korner or Kurt's Kold Kuts. Yes, intentionally, with three Ks.

Before leaving home, I'd always make sure I had a full tank of gas. I was driving about 80 miles each way and wanted to avoid running out. One morning however, I was rushing and had just enough gas to get to work, but barely enough to get out of the old ghost town. I'd have to stop at the gas station a couple blocks from the clinic at some point during the day.

Around one in the afternoon, I headed over to the gas station. Outside of getting some glares for very obviously being out of place in my brown skin, everything was fine. The small town gas pump ticked along drably as I stood in the sun, thankful for the respite from the clinic's icy air conditioning.

As I pumped, I suddenly heard music blaring from down the road. I turned to look and saw a red pickup truck decorated with a Confederate flag waving confidently. If only such symbols came with some disclaimer underneath, maybe a miniature flag that read something like, "ignorant Southern pride" or "just plain ole' hateful." There were a couple of guys in the back, yelling over the music, but I couldn't make out what they were saying. They came to an abrupt, screeching stop at the intersection where the gas station sat. I held my breath.

No eye contact, I told myself. I waited, staring at the slow-moving gas pump indicator as the numbers flipped as lazily as anything would on a hot summer day. I clutched the handle as tight as I could. Nothing changed. In fact, the numbers seemed to somehow move even slower. The men hollered some more, maybe at me, maybe at each other, leaving behind a trail of profanity as they skidded off.

I sucked in a deep breath of stifling air, surprised by the many what-ifs that ran through my mind in those few short seconds. I was surprised by my own reaction to a red flag with a couple of sinister lines and lackluster stars.

I'm often surprised at the luck of those who don't even flinch when they see that flag, and in fact, some justify it, while others endorse and protect it. Because to them it means freedom.

What Sharing Privilege Looks Like

A teenage girl came in for psychological services. Like most young people, she was guarded at first, but eventually began talking about a difficult past riddled with cruelty followed by abandonment. She cried at times, ensuring to avert eye contact. Teenagers are so hard to reach, I was glad she felt she could share. We laughed together a little near the end of the session, often a relieving sign of a glimmer of hope. But even still, there was something unsettling about her.

She missed her follow-up appointment. I hoped she would return soon. The heaviness she carried shouldn't have to be contained in such a young life. As weeks passed, I wondered how she was doing and whether anyone was helping her hold her pain, and whether someone, even just one person, told her she was loved.

Then one day, just like that, she was back. As I was scanning the waiting area to check on another client's arrival, I saw the girl sitting with shoulders hunched and staring into her hands. After wrapping up some paperwork, I headed over to the waiting area to call her in.

But before I could open the door, my colleague, Julia, stopped me. "I'm sorry, the client said she didn't want to see the 'dark one.' I'm so sorry that some people are *that* ignorant." I wasn't naive. I was working in the hometown of a former grand dragon of the KKK, but it did feel a little like I was kicked in the stomach.

As I was walking through the waiting area a while later, I saw the young lady standing at the reception desk with an older man. He glanced my way and instantly began throwing looks of disgust at me, as though he was a cyborg programmed to do so.

The girl watched this silent interaction and eventually began to mimic him.

Her gaze was unlike his piercing and defiant stare. Hers was filled with deep emptiness. I walked away wondering if she even knew why she thought she loathed me. The lines between sadness and anger, fear and hate are so very thin.

I almost felt defeated. She was too young to despise anyone, but I suppose she was also too impressionable not to. She was vulnerable in many ways, one of those being that she didn't yet have her own sense of self-worth, so how could she accept anyone else?

I say I *almost* felt defeated because knowing that Julia knew exactly what to say, exactly what I needed to hear, was the buffer. It was the hope that one day more people will be reasonable, less intolerant. She validated my disappointment that it's a tragedy to feel this girl is unreachable right now. She acknowledged that this was a case of hate having had won.

That one statement was a million consoling words for me. Julia could have said, "Oh, that's just how it is around here," or "She's young," or "She didn't mean it that way." But instead, she called it out for the vile thing it was. Hate begets hate.

And what hurt most was that the girl was somewhere around 15-years-old. She wasn't 70 and stuck in a different era, still calling people of color negroes or coloreds like some of my patients had. This was taught to her, passed down from those 70-year-olds, and onto 40-year-olds, and now onto her impressionable young mind, once pure, as God created it. Through generations, she was given the gift of hate.

Although it was disappointing, it was a little easier to face knowing Julia was aligned with me. She was aligned despite it not happening to her, despite having no direct impact from it, despite her being white and being completely unaffected, if she chose to see it that way. But she chose otherwise. She didn't have to sacrifice anything to align with me. She didn't have to move aside and relinquish her privilege. She was simply human in all its beauty—willing to hold my disappointment alongside me.

This is what sharing privilege looks like.

Grief of a Female Immigrant

You recognize what that bright, radiant smile means when you look into a woman's eyes as she's walking down the street. Knowingly, you then glance down at a little version of her, joyfully skipping along beside her, their hands clasped together.

My mother lacked that radiant smile. Although she may have felt the delight of motherhood just the same, she expressed it as a burden. She had bigger things to worry about besides enjoying a stroll with her daughter. She had to protect her little girl. She had too many fears and much confusion about what America did to people.

She wasn't warm, but instead practical. Everything offended her, but nothing penetrated her enough to really hurt. She just did what she had to do to push through the complications that were her life in America.

As I got older, I also realized that she once lived in a country where little girls were a high commodity, not to be bought or sold - well sometimes that, too - but mostly to just be taken and freely preyed upon, even unworthy of a transaction.

When my mother and I walked down the street, she kept me close, very close. She gripped my squirmy 4-year-old hand tightly as we took harried walks around the neighborhood. I treasured them. I was ignorant to her bizarre vigilance. I noticed her eyes darting around compulsively and didn't think anything of it. But when I remember those times now, she'd never respond the first time I asked her a question. "Mom, can we go to the candy store and get ring pops? Mom? Mom?"

I thought it was because she was focusing on carefully crossing the street or something. I knew she cared about that a lot. Once, she spanked me pretty bad because I couldn't remember which way I was supposed to look first before crossing the street. Left first.

I relished the years when she retained a semblance of a secret sparkle in her eyes on good days, something that she was too stoic to ever express freely no matter how content. Yet, she tried to communicate with me the best she knew how, through ambiguous symbols and riddles, spankings and reprimands, letting me know she was standing by, even if uncomfortably.

Mom was only eighteen when I was born so I became her sidekick on her rare days off of work from the nursing home. Some mornings, we went to breakfast. Sometimes, we went to the local taqueria and played "The Tide is High" on the jukebox over and over again.

Even if we couldn't afford to have a full lunch, she'd buy me a taco so we could listen to Blondie swoon over a light, tropical melody. The restaurant was usually pretty empty in the late afternoon, and Mom would let me slide out of the booth and dance while my puffy, bright frock swayed back and forth to the beat. She giggled with satisfaction, despite her hunger.

From time to time, she'd come by my kindergarten class and lightly knock at the window to get my attention. Oddly, no one else seemed to notice or maybe they decided it was best to ignore the strange lady lurking outside. It was a time before mass school shootings and assuming any vaguely Middle Eastern looking person was a terrorist.

Mom flashed a small smile and a couple minutes later, busted me out of class with a half assed and harried, "She has a doctor's appointment and she's late," excuse for the teacher, emphasizing the "late" as though it was my teacher's fault. Those days, I guess you didn't have to go to an office and talk to a grumpy attendance lady first. Or maybe you did. Mom often scoffed at procedures. "There's no lines bines, in India." She whisked me straight past the main office and quickly out of the front door so we could have a day of impromptu window-shopping.

It was as though she did it all on an impulse while sitting at home agonizing over something she didn't want to think about. Shopping was one of the only things that could put her into a peaceful lull.

No matter where we went, she never took her eyes off of me. And when someone walked into a store and especially down the same aisle we were shopping in, she scolded me to stay close and gripped my hand so tightly that it folded within itself like origami. Even though she obsessively reviewed the dangers of crossing the street or to be hypervigilantly aware of all the creepy things that lurk in alleys, she stood watching as I walked the few blocks to school and made that left turn into the school playground.

On the city bus, she'd sit up real straight with one leg sticking out into the aisle like she was positioning to bounce out of her seat and lunge at someone within zero to three seconds, if she had to. Almost nothing could distract her from keeping me in her Special Forces security detail visual grip.

One snowy afternoon when I was about six, Mom zipped me into my snug one-piece snowsuit and we made the trek to some store on the crowded city bus. I can't remember what the destination was because the events of the bus ride there overtook that day's space in my brain.

As the bus moved along bumpily, I tried to divert my mind from the thick, puffy snowsuit that was now making me sweaty and giving off the funk of gym shoes sitting at the bottom of a backpack. I had a piece of butterscotch candy in my mouth and was captured by the smooth coin-like roundedness of its texture, and the richness of the buttery flavoring. I switched the almost quarter-sized candy from cheek to cheek to renew its sweetness. I then hid it under my tongue to see how that might change the taste and to even just find out if it would fit. I held it between my teeth as I glided my tongue on the ridge of it. Finally, as it began dissolving and shrinking, I allowed it to happily settle on the top of my tongue as I sucked on it.

    I was sitting in the row in front of my mother staring out of the large bus window. I was in the middle of pretending I was gliding through the air while sitting on a magical elephant, when the bus abruptly rolled over a bump that made the passengers jerk forward in their seats and collectively gasp. I usually loved the bumps on bus rides because they gave me that kinda bouncy, kinda queasy feeling in the pit of my stomach, like a carnival roller coaster.

    Except this time was different. The butterscotch had disappeared. I tried to gasp for air. I leapt up from my seat in a panic and began flailing my arms. I stumbled toward Mom who was sitting in the seat behind me. I pointed to my mouth to tell her I couldn't breathe and only zombie-like wheezing sounds screeched out.

Mom seemed irritated and commanded me to get a hold of myself. "Stop being silly and sit before you fall." She glanced toward the front of the bus as she stuck her hand out toward the driver and said, "Don't you see he's crazy. Sit down!" Finally, she returned her eyes toward me and realized that something was very wrong.

She shot desperate glances around the bus, looking for someone who might know what to do. She jumped out of her seat and pleaded for someone to help. She demanded. She screamed. "Please, my daughter is choking. She can't breathe. Please, somebody help her." She continued to glance franticly around the bus as tears seemed to blur her vision. This might've been one of the few times in my childhood that I remember my mother reaching out to an American stranger for help. This was maybe the first time she sought direct eye contact from any unfamiliar person.

A very tall, brown, maybe Native American man somehow decoded every syllable of her terror-stricken glance and quickly jumped into action. He performed the Heimlich confidently and systematically as if he knew he was placed on the bus to do this exact thing. "Okay, brave girl, it's okay. Spit it out. One." Pressure between the sternum and belly button. "Two." More intense pressure. I started to feel hopeless and confused about why I couldn't breathe and simultaneously wondered why this big man was touching me in this way. I could remember thinking too that my mom was probably standing in a karate chop stance behind the man ready to attack because he was touching me. A million times she told me, "Never let anyone touch you." I heard her voice echo in my mind now as I gasped for air. So why wasn't she stopping him? "And three. Great job!" he sang as the butterscotch grazed my throat, making its dramatic exit from my mouth and onto the already sticky bus floor.

With my hands on my wobbly knees, I took in several quick short breaths between coughs, coaxing my lungs to clear. He proceeded to pat me on the back heartily with his large hands as though he expected butterscotch remnants to continue to come spewing out in tiny bits. It dawned on me that he saved my life and that Mom wasn't angry with him at all. She was thankful. Once my breathing regulated, the man gave me a warm, sincere hug that wasn't frightening but instead, surprisingly comforting.

This. It took this to make her reach out to other people, to see them as safe, not bad men or women, not thieves or liars, not those damn Americans, even if for that moment.

Black Magic

In a gossipy whisper she said, "Maybe he put that black magic on her, you know?"

"Did your friend *really* say that, Mom? Black magic?" What a dumb ass thing to say. And it's not even appropriately racist. It's just weird.

"Yes, so shocking. She really said that," Mom replied. "So stu-pid," annunciating the word with so much frustration and with such a thick Indian accent that it almost sounded like she was spitting and speaking at the same time.

"Does your friend even know what black magic is?"

This is what happens after your mother's zealously curious friends find out about your secret black boyfriend. Ignorance ensues.

When people are not seen as people, and instead, voodoo masters who randomly place mystical spells on others, it is easier to create a distance between us and the *stripped from humanity* oddity that becomes them. It creates a portal for ignorance by concocting ridiculousness such as the bizarrely used term "black magic."

Unusual nonhuman characteristics can then be easily layered onto these assumptions to create the most fantastical mythological creatures, far beyond what our fears have caused us to imagine. Humans can be metamorphosed into that mysterious unknown thing until reduced to behaving as beasts. It is the thing that slavery was made of.

People go to great lengths of imagination to make divisions. And in this case, it was done with the highest allegiance to ignorance. But what can I expect? These are people who considered themselves far more superior than others, a typical defense for people who feel they have severe shortcomings to hide.

So asking folks such as that to see a person for who he is, is asking far too much. So I didn't. In fact, I didn't give even a teeny weeny shit about what the wannabe elitists thought because, well, as my life motto goes for situations such as this, "It doesn't change my life any."

Other, bigger things would in fact impact my life though, like knowing my family is well, like being who I am, like loving who I want.

Spirals

Those damn Asians.

Those damn Asian Indians.

Those damn Asian South Indians.

Those damn Asian South Indian Christians.

Those damn Asian South Indian Telugu speaking Christians.

Those damn Asian South Indian Telugu speaking Christians from Hyderabad.

Those damn Asian South Indian Telugu speaking Christians from Hyderabad who live in the country.

Those damn Asian South Indian Telugu speaking Christians from Hyderabad who live in the country with less money than us.

Those damn dark-skinned Asian South Indian Telugu speaking Christians from Hyderabad who live in the country with less money than us.

We start in one self-prescribed group and because we're so desperate to make ourselves feel taller and stronger and more important than we feel inside, we divide more and more until we're broken. And then we keep going even further still until one day, we realize that there's no one else. There isn't even an echo.

We Are Conquistadors!

I did it! Actually, *we* did it. There could be no other way. You, my dear, were the reason they were finally willing to understand the world as it should be seen.

When my parents came to America, they brought with them a few belongings, some big dreams and a host of misconceptions about what the people of America were like. In fact, they seemed to see non-Indians in a grossly inaccurate, almost cartoonish light.

Ironically, when I think of their perceptions, they parallel to Americans' views of Apu from The Simpsons. He's a clownish little Indian man with a heavy accent and unethical business practices. In the same vein, my parents saw all Americans as sex crazed hippies with no concept of collectivism, family and sacrifice. Above all, Americans lacked any desire to maintain an untainted reputation, regardless of the costs.

It makes some sense. They would be encountering so many people unlike themselves that they had to create a sort of blueprint for understanding the many puzzle pieces that made up America. This can be useful to a point I suppose, but it was also quite harmful. It drew lines between the perceived stark differences separating Indians and "the others."

My parents were unable to relinquish how their custom-laden world could even vaguely line up with any strand of American culture. And further, meshing even slightly with the recklessly liberal nature of Americans would be treason of Indian culture.

Had my parents considered though that their children were born into this sin, and may one day adopt some of these dreaded qualities? Well, no. Not for a long, long time, not until they had to face you, my very non-prescribed boyfriend. Until then, they held on tight to their misinformed notions, which sometimes unwittingly teetered on the brink of intolerance.

And so when you came along, the concept of *us* was incomprehensible to them, a paradox. But slowly they began to bend. The change was so subtle that it almost went undetected. It was in the small interactions – silence replaced by laughter, formalities replaced by meaningful exchanges – that they were being redefined. They needed you. They needed light. They needed exposure and reflection of their own vulnerabilities.

We did this! We pushed them out of their uncomfortable places. We showed them something they had never dreamt of. We, my love, are conquistadors!

Part III: Ground Me Without Stepping on My Mind

Oppression begins at a very early age in some families. From birth, girls must relinquish any notion of authority. Growing up, her father is her superior, the head of the house. When she marries, her husband reigns over her. If she births a son, she must quietly endure her lack of stature in the family because he, too, will hold authority over his compliant mother after the death of his father.

The ever-intuitive mother who guides her children persistently, anticipates her husband's needs before they are a thought in his mind, and wakes first and lies down far after everyone else is cozily dreaming - she is the one who is apparently of no worth.

And then there's church folk, with the wife sitting in the pew with sweat beads ornamenting her hairline but wearing a scarf over her head, because somebody says the Bible says she must. Her husband sits next to her, taking up most of the seat with his legs spread comfortably and arms draped leisurely over the back of the seat.

And then he sits up even taller and stretches out a little further when the preacher man starts talking in his fake authoritative voice and says, "Well, the Bible says, 'Wives, submit to your husbands,'" and then clears his throat because he knows he's preaching lies.

Contrary to popular and cynical belief and the ease of omission, I Corinthians 11:11-12 also reads, "Men, submit to your wives." It further states, "Nevertheless, in the Lord woman is not independent of man nor man of woman; for as woman was made from man, so man is now born of woman. And all things are from God." It's interesting that few people for whom "Women, submit to your husbands," is advantageous somehow fail to provide full disclosure.

Society's mandates, self-appointed masters and preposterous customs mindlessly passed forward are what allegedly dictate life, while God is ignored and females silenced.

Yet good sir, it is said we were born out of your side. Uphold me and I too will stand by you. Know that if you are able to ground me without stepping on my mind, we will be something magnificent.

Being the Wrong Kind

So they tell me that when I was born, my father didn't want to see me. My only infraction was that I was a girl. He denies it. Of course he would. I wonder what that was like, if it was true. I picture him walking into the nursery, looking at the little plastic containers holding people's joys and burdens. He must have read names like Smith, Johnson, Walters, before he got to me.

I wonder if he did a double take. Did he look at my name, hopes real high, and then look at it again more carefully with squinted, disappointed eyes? Did he think he misread Patricia for Patrick? I'm told I was very fair as a baby, often mistaken for Mexican or some blend of white and something. Did he maybe think they labeled me wrong and I was switched with this other strange little baby girl?

Did he ever really want me? And how would things be different if I were a boy? That treasured first-born boy? And what inadequacies is he disappointed about beyond the ones I already know of?

He tried so hard to make me fit. I grew up fixing things, like rigging our TV so we could change channels, sweating over instructions on how to assemble desks and tables, pushing along our manual lawnmower in the blazing sun and piling up fresh snow half as tall as me onto the edges of sidewalks on dreary winter evenings.

But this didn't exempt me from doing all the things required of girls in a typical Indian family. I was the dishwasher, the older sister commanded to care for her younger siblings. I fed them, changed them. I couldn't spend time with friends because after all, I had two young children to help care for. And if I went out, who would get my baby brother to fall asleep? "You're the only one who can put him to sleep," Mom fussed. It was true. So naturally, I tended to my obligations.

Can't say it didn't build character. Otherwise, how would I know how to kick-start a lazy sub pump when it rained or effectively bring down high fevers in toddlers? Yet, despite my skills and all my show of responsibility, it still didn't change the reality that I couldn't go out with friends after 9 pm or sometimes at all, even as an older teenager.

Even in high school, I was forbidden from having contact with males, including classmates just calling for missed homework. Having male classmates was clearly not under my control. Through Dad's gritted teeth, stupendously fluffy mustache and mumbled accent, classmates would get cursed out if they dared dial my number. Luckily, my classmates often couldn't make out what was said. They just knew the phone call was over because Dad hung up on them mid-sentence.

Every Sunday, we went to a fashion show that everybody called church. And I was the highly reluctant and agitated model, donning the type of heavy, draped clothes that required that I shuffled sideways like a zombie out of the Thriller video to walk. I had to wear bangles up to my armpits and all kinds of excessive ornaments in my hair and ears, everything held together in a delicate balance by millions of bobby pins. Sometimes the hair and ear jewelry even connected.

I often fantasized about protesting the bombastic outfits. And I finally got up the nerve around the age of 16. But because I wasn't as brave as I pretended I was, I didn't walk out of my room in my purple suede Pumas, jeans and three sizes too big flannel shirt on Sunday mornings. Instead, I'd oblige my parents by wearing some blindingly loud outfit.

But I kept wearing the same outfit every, single, week. Like a uniform.

That is, until they caught on like three weeks later, and started calling me all kinds of Lucifers and demons, and threatened to have me exorcised, as they demanded I find another outfit. So my version of backing off was to switch to another uniform for about another three weeks, until they noticed that I needed holy oil and a crucifix again.

I had all kinds of protesting going on. And why not? I was the wrong kind. What would ever be good enough? I couldn't magically become a boy. I couldn't un-disappoint anyone. I could simply try to live my life while partially appeasing them.

Yet that too, doesn't work when you start off being the wrong kind and then further wrong others, just by being you. The older I got, the more American I got, at least in my parents' perspective. Despite their reassurance on my first day of kindergarten that I was an "American, just like everybody else," I was now far too American for their liking. "You're Indian," they'd now yell. "Be Indian." I couldn't un-be American, nor could I un-be Indian, so there was that conundrum.

I just was. And I kept on just being that. I don't know if I've ever been too American or too Indian, but I'm some and most of both. I don't know where the dividing line begins or if there is one.

And also, as for the first problem, I'm still a girl. I'm not a guy. I'm a bit boyish, though. Does that count? I surely don't understand the concept of bobby pins or why people arch their eyebrows. In fact, I think the latter is sadistic, without benefits. Also, it doesn't change the face at all, not even a little.

I wonder sometimes if my boyish ways developed because Dad wished I were one. Even despite his alleged disappointment, maybe he decided he would work with what he had. And the older I get, the more I question this disappointment I've been told about, especially because I can remember following him around like a little duckling everywhere he went.

"Patty, let's go to the store." He'd say, "Come with me to the laundromat," his accent pushing him to drag the "o." I'd just wait for the invitation, because going to the laun-drooooo-mat with Dad was like going to the carnival. He'd make up silly games as we waited for the clothes to wash. When they were done, we'd toss a shirt or sock around pretending it was a ball. Folding clothes was my favorite though because we'd race to see who could fold the most.

It's funny sometimes, how when he sees that I'm dressed for comfort even at a more formal event or when I roll my eyes at the impracticality of shopping for any given item for more than twenty minutes, he laughs. Then, with a look that's something like pride, he says, "You're so much like me."

The Symbiosis of Dowry

Although a dynamic concept, the word symbiosis comes down to one main definition: obligation. It brings to mind the custom of dowry. Dowry in fact, counters the true concept of mutual symbiosis, where both organisms benefit from each other. Instead, the very act of dowry annihilates any chance of mutuality and quite blatantly establishes the power advantage of males.

Actually, the concept of dowry would fit more appropriately in another subcategory of symbiosis. Parasitic symbiosis is when one organism benefits from the other just as a parasite takes from its unsuspecting host. Parasitic symbiosis leaves the host with no concept of self at all.

I can hear the voices of some of the older women saying, "Oh, you're being dramatic. It's our culture, a long-established tradition. Traditions are not made to be broken." Aren't they?

And sure, dowry traditions are not always practiced in nefarious ways. Some families may follow dowry customs simply because it's what's always been done. They mean no purposeful ill intent to the bride.

Marriage is naturally a momentous time across many cultures, but it may be the pinnacle of the lifespan in highly traditional Indian families. It is everything parents work toward. It is the event in which a child is taught to invest all hopes and visions for the future. Picture a young man whose gleeful parents plan excitedly. The boy conjures up visions of a beautiful and useful bride as his parents busily make phone calls, notifying their relatives and friends that, "It is time." Those phone calls are like tentacles reaching for all potential marrying age women.

Once the selection is narrowed down, the two families meet. The patient young woman studies the carpeted floor intently, head bowed to avoid eye contact as a show of respect. She listens on as though she is a spectator, while negotiations between the parents of the potential bride and groom intensify, the most contentious point being the material price of the lovely bride's worth.

Her parents speak about her rare qualities. They share about her expertise in household tasks. They boast about her character. She has such kindness, patience and an especially long-suffering nature, they say. They rave of her endurance to give and give without expecting reciprocity. They marvel at her innate abilities to care for her younger siblings. Surely, she will make an ideal mother, they boast.

The woman shifts uncomfortably in her seat, expression unreadable, but eyes revealing her bewilderment as she quickly glances at her potential groom, wondering how she will bring herself to bear children with a man she finds undesirable. Although he's physically attractive just fine, it's her utter indifference toward him that frightens her. She senses this glorious future her parents anticipate for her will be replaced by a hollow gaping hole in her being.

Once all costs and benefits of the arrangement are painstakingly weighed, the bride's parents display profuse gratitude before leaving, the bride only having spoken twice, when greeting the family and bidding them farewell.

All that these loving parents are really seeking for their children are a capable husband for their daughter and a good wife for their son. It's innocent. The groom's intent is not to subjugate his bride or exert his authority over her. He doesn't want to, but it's there regardless. It's there because the archaic custom of dowry continues to exist, and its very existence symbolizes the power a man has over a woman.

Ultimately, it symbolizes the act of a woman's family offering a gift to the groom's family for taking a girl off of her parents' hands. It implies that the bride should be compliant with the terms of the negotiations. She is expected to be whatever the contractual obligations state she should be, in whatever form that may be. Is a woman so burdensome an affliction that her family must offer compensation to be relieved of her?

So see, even if done under the facade of custom and even if seen as naively benign, the practice will always symbolize malicious intent. It will always represent the parasite's desire to exert authority and take from his host whatever he wishes.

Grandma's Bad Ass Tattoo

"Nana Amma, I'm sleepy. I don't wanna go to school," I complained. As always, Grandma was ready with some magical, mythical remedy. "Okay, then do this, do this, and do this," she said in her heavy Indian accent, with "this" pronounced more like "dis." She touched her feet then slowly straightened up and placed her arms out to her sides for a couple of seconds.

She threw me a, "Don't just stand there" look," so I got into sync, mimicking every move. For the last stretch, we raised our arms over our heads. As she brought her arms down, I noticed a tattoo of a leaf on the inside of her thin, brown wrist. "Nana Amma, what's that?" I pointed toward her arm. She laughed bashfully, or was it shamefully, and changed the subject.

Nana Amma came to live with us when I was

12 years old. My grandpa, Tha Tha, died suddenly a few months before, so my parents thought Nana Amma could use a change of environment. Getting to know Nana Amma was unexpectedly fascinating.

Her stories of India weren't simply stories. They were teleportation. I only visited India once when I was four, and hearing Nana Amma's stories was like a million magical rides. They reconnected me to people who were like ghosts in my mind. They were fading childhood memories, growing fainter with time, that is, until she took me with her on her journeys.

Nana Amma taught me about Indian culture in a way that my parents couldn't. Mom and Dad had to put their culture aside, subdue it while at work or around non-Indians, as though it was a terrible family secret. I'd watch as they'd attempt to modify their thick accents, soften their r's and t's when they spoke with Americans. They'd shorten their vowels, which they'd much rather drag out, curl, twist and thump. Behind closed doors, they were far more intentional, flamboyant even, with labored, thick annunciation of each syllable. They were chameleons. But Nana Amma, she lived freely here, never questioning who she was. She seemed to bask in the ease of knowing what being Indian meant.

It just recently occurred to me that Nana Amma's morning stretches were very likely yoga moves that she learned as a child, maybe from her parents. According to Dad, my great-grandparents followed Hindu religion, but later converted to Christianity.

Well, maybe converted isn't the best way to put it. At some point in my ancestors' lives, some people who had no business showing up in my great-grandparents' village decided to show up in my great-grandparents' village. The uninvited were very different from the villagers, most apparently, their radiant, white, God-like skin.

It seems the new people were stealthy in their ability to ambush the village in a, "Well, I wouldn't necessarily call it *that*" type of way. Based on the stories told to my father, the new people coolly pointed out what was wrong with our culture and went about matter-of-factly changing it. It was a well-implemented transition, so much so that the people of the village somehow came to adore the people with the white skin instead of revolting against them. And in fact, the people of the village began to feel ashamed of the things they believed before, the food they prepared, their exercise and meditation practices, their golden brown skin and the formerly proud body markings of their tribal allegiance.

Each morning, I wake up, sleepily stumble into the bathroom, and stand in front of the mirror. I take in a deep breath. I reach my arms far above my head. I hold them out to the side. I touch my curled toes for a couple seconds. I then gingerly run a finger over the tattoo that now sits on the inside of my thin, brown arm. I stretch my neck and look up to heaven. *For you, Nana Amma, I will wear it without shame.*

The Chai Alchemist

How do you know when to stop pouring the milk? When in an even and consistent mood, you could measure it out, of course. But more often, taken by wild rapture, there's something magical about stopping at just the right and unforeseen moment. The color becomes a delicate creamy caramel, or chocolatey as though it has long basked in the glorious sun. Other times it more closely matches a shade of coffee swirling with slowly poured cream.

The consistency is perfection as it develops within a slow rolling tumble, and then violent and commanding boil, nearly bursting over the rim of its restraining steel container. Somewhat frothy and thick, but the completion of its luscious touch is not visibly known alone. The presence of all senses must stand at attention to reach its true and exquisite nature. Hints of earth colored clove and olive cardamom dance around the senses with light, agile feet.

It's lovely, even magnificent as it sways. It's ready to be poured into its vessel. This brown elixir of vast spectrums, it is complete now. This robust, perplexing and spectacular brown, she is beautiful.

Acknowledgements

My beloved ladybugs, Naomi and Imani, you are my light and my inspiration. For KJ, the one who my soul loves, thank you for grounding me. I adore you forever and for always because you are my dear ones.

Thank you Reena Chili and Raju Mama for all things all the time. Thanks Mom and Dad for hopefully not disowning me after you read this. Thank you, God, for always reminding me to be still and know that you got me.

www.ingramcontent.com/pod-product-compliance
Lightning Source LLC
Chambersburg PA
CBHW061656040426
42446CB00010B/1757